WOMEN ORIENTATED LAW: CONSEQUENCES FACE BY MALES

VOLUME 1, ISSUE 4 OF BRILLOPEDIA

ALVEENA SIDDIQUI

ISBN 979-888546003-3

Contents

Preface   *v*

Author   *vii*

Publication   *ix*

  1. Abstract   1

  2. Introduction   2

  3. Laws Only In Favour Of Women In Which Men Are Excluded   4

  4. Dowry Death   5

  5. Maintenance Of Wife By The Husband   6

  6. False Dowry Cases   8

  7. Domestic Violence   9

  8. Reasons Why Domestic Violence Cases Against Men Go   11
     Unreported

  9. Maintenance Of Wife By The Husband   13

10. Sexual Assault Against Men(Non- Centrical Law)   14

11. Is "rape Is Patriarchal" ?   17

12. Gender Neutrality Of Rape Laws   20

13. How Men Can Cloak?   23

14. Conclusions   25

Preface

"Start writing, no matter what. The water does not flow until the faucet is turned on".

-Louis L'Amour

Hundreds of students and professors are contributing their work to Brillopedia, we are here to provide ample information about Law and Contemporary issues. Our aim is to provide a platform for today's generation to express their views and ideas on law and contemporary law.

Author

Alveena Siddiqui

Publication

This research paper is published in volume 1, issue 4 of Brillopedia

CHAPTER ONE

ABSTRACT

"When people get used to preferential treatment, equal treatment seems like discrimination."

-Thomas Sowell

The Indian upbringing of a man has created a stereotype that a man can never feel pain, and if he does, he is not a man. The same belief has led to people believing that a man cannot be raped or sexually assaulted because men are privileged to be men in a patriarchal society. Men are often or always believed to be the perpetrators of sexual assault and not the victim, whereas, in the case of women, it is believed that women can only be victims and never the perpetrators. Just because men are expected to be tough and strong, doesn't mean that they don't face challenges that women face in their daily lives. While we talk about the rights of women, we shouldn't ignore the rights of men. The goal is to empower the women, not neglect the other gender in order to uplift the other. <u>Focusing only on one gender</u> is injustice, unfair and violative of the fundamental rights of people under Article 14 and 15 of the Constitution of India.

CHAPTER TWO

INTRODUCTION

Women orientated laws are made to benefit women who are considered as an oppressed section of the society. But there is a need to see these laws from a different perspective. These laws are affecting the rights of the males who are being harassed by a false charge against them. The role of the judiciary is to provide justice to every individual and there can be no discrimination between men and women when it comes to justice. Even if one innocent is tried or loses his life, it is a big stigma on the women orientated laws.

Rape or sexual assault of men and boys have been kept a "Dark Secret" for so long that now the society is either oblivious to this or completely turns a blind eye towards such incidents if they ever come out of the shadow. The social pressure, fear of being disbelieved and social backlash stop the male victims of sexual assault from opening up to anyone about these difficult and painful incidents, encouraging the perpetrators to go on hunting their prey. Judging from the findings of a recent Economic Times-Synovate survey, the men need to be incorporated in that bill ASAP. Of the 527 people queried across seven cities – Bangalore, Chennai, Delhi, Hyderabad, Kolkata, Mumbai and Pune – 19% said they have faced some kind of sexual harassment at office. In Bangalore, 51% of the respondents had been sexually harassed, while in Delhi and Hyderabad, 31% and 28% of those surveyed said they had been sexually harassed. Around 38% of the respondents across 7 cities in India said that in today's workplaces, "men are as vulnerable to sexual harassment as women."[1] The biggest reason why these cases were never reported was "social ridicule" and because they felt they wouldn't be believed due to India's social beliefs

Data shows that maximum males commit suicide due to mental trauma which they suffer from because of false allegations charged by their female counterparts than the stress of workloads or any other reasons. Sec. 498-A,

376 of IPC, 1860 and sec. 125 of CrPC, 1973 have been mostly used by females to humiliate men. These legislations are made by Parliament to protect the women from any kind exploitation but the result of this had backfired and women themselves started humiliating males. This can be the main reason that introducing legislation against marital rape is still a debatable topic

[1] Rape in India, Wikipedia, https://en.wikipedia.org/wiki/Rape_in_India

CHAPTER THREE

LAWS ONLY IN FAVOUR OF WOMEN IN WHICH MEN ARE EXCLUDED

Laws should be made for protection of all the individuals but ,by INDIAN Constitution Article 15(3)- State can make law in favour of women and children,

Constitutional Privileges

(Article 15) Prohibition of discrimination on grounds of religion, race, caste, sex or place of birth.

(Article 15(1))The State shall not discrimination against any citizen on grounds only of religion, race, caste, sex, or place of birth or any of them.

(Article 15(3)) The State to make any special provision in favour of women and children

(Article 51(A) (e)) is related to women. It states that;

It shall be the duty of every citizen of India to promote harmony and the spirit of common brotherhood amongst all the people of India transcending religion, linguistic, regional or sectional diversities; to renounce practices derogatory to the dignity of women.

Article 243 D (3) and Article 243 T(3) provide for reservation of not less than one third of total number of seats in Panchayats and Municipalities for women to be allotted by rotation to different Constituencies.

Article 243 D(4) T(4) provides that not less than one third of the total number of officers of chairperson in the Panchayat and Municipalities at each level to be reserved for women.[2]

CHAPTER FOUR

Dowry death

<u>Section 304-B</u> of IPC is a provision made to protect the women from cruelty by her husband and in-laws for dowry. It is presumed that if a woman dies within seven years of her marriage and her husband or in-laws were demanding dowry, then they were responsible for her sudden death. This provision protects women but what about men. There is no such rule that if a husband dies within seven years of marriage the wife can be held liable.

- The Indian Constitution
- Dowry Prohibition Act 1961

The law should be such that which protects the rights of each and everyone in the society and not only the females. Also, a proper enquiry should be there about the reason for the death of the women and not directly putting the blame on the husband and the in-laws as the assailant.

CHAPTER FIVE

Maintenance of wife by the husband

<u>Section 125</u> of the <u>Code of Criminal Procedure, 1973</u> mentions that a person is supposed to maintain his wife, children and his parents who are unable to maintain themselves. Even if the wife earns, that income is not enough to support her and the husband has to provide for her needs.

<u>Section 37</u> of the Special Marriage Act provides that the husband has to maintain his wife from his property after divorce until there is a change in her circumstances like she is remarried or has turned immoral.

<u>Section 18</u> of the Hindu Adoption and Maintenance Act states that a Hindu wife has a right to be maintained by her husband throughout her lifetime

<u>Section 3</u> of the <u>Muslim Women(Protection of Rights on Divorce) Act, 1986</u> states that a divorced Muslim woman is entitled to be maintained by her ex-husband during the period of iddat.

<u>Section 37</u> of the <u>Divorce Act, 1869</u> provides that the husband has to provide maintenance to his wife throughout her life when a decree of dissolution or decree of judicial separation is passed.

These all laws which are mentioned above provide for the maintenance of a wife by her husband but no provisions are there which talk about a husband being maintained by his wife. There may be a situation where the husband can also need maintenance but that criteria is not provided in the above-discussed provisions. In Family Law, a wife is supported when it comes to divorce and maintenance. <u>Section 125</u> of CrPC provides that if the husband is unable to provide for the maintenance of his wife, a warrant may be issued against him for recovery. Even when it comes to the custody of a child, preferably it is the wife who receives it for at least the child who is below 5 years of age. In adoption cases too, a single male is not allowed to adopt a female child. These all laws have loopholes which affect the males drastically.

CHAPTER SIX

False dowry cases

This is the most critical situation these days. Law take strict actions against the one taking or supporting dowry. This was one of the best thing done until and unless women started misusing the law in their favour. Women these days often register false dowry cases to threaten her husband and his family and also to get benefits of her marital life. The sad part is there are rarely cases where a men can prove his innocence and mostly is found guilty despite of doing nothing. Though, the law in many states have made changes to verify whether a man is accused of such case.

In case of Dr. N.G. Dastane Vs. S. Dastane[1], SC held that although physical cruelty is presumed to be done mainly by husband being the powerful but mental cruelty can be done by both husband and wife. Even wife can do mental cruelty on husband.

In case of Anil Bharadwaj Vs. Nimlesh Bharadwaj[2], court held that if a wife refuses to have sexual intercourse with her husband without any reasonable cause will amount to cruelty.

False rape and other charges

Usually, in rape cases women are considered to be the victim and there are high chances of women getting the case in favour. If a women reports a rape case, the culprit will immediately be taken into custody and will anyhow be looked down in a society as Indian people stands for rape victims. Taking advantage of the strong feminism movement, there are women who report false rape cases intending to take revenge or any such grudges etc. and thus many innocent men has to face punishment for things they did not do. Also, their whole life is a taint. Some even prefer to end up with their life.

[1] AIR 1975 1534

[2] AIR 1987 Delhi 111, ILR 1986 Delhi 383

CHAPTER SEVEN

Domestic violence

The laws which are mostly misused are Section 498-A and Section 376of Indian Penal Code. Section 498-Aof IPC deals with the subjugation of women to cruelty by her husband or her in-laws. The first point that the IPC nowhere mentions about, is the cruelty towards men which is also a possibility. It is not necessary that only women can be subjected to cruelty but some of them are capable of subjecting men to cruelty too. IPC mentions cruelty by men and not by a person which can cover within its ambit both men and women. When the woman or her relative's file complaint in the police station, an action is taken against the husband immediately. The husband, along with his family members, can be put behind the bars for 3 years and fine.

It is a non-bailable, cognizable (the police officer can arrest without warrant) and non-compoundable (a complaint cannot be compounded just by withdrawing the case but has to be quashed by the High Court) offence. Also, the public view in such cases is that the husband is the one who is guilty and mostly the decisions in such cases are in favour of the women.

The tears of females are visible to everyone but no one sees the tears of men. There are so many false cases of domestic violence being lodged and innocent people are being put behind the bars. The family of the husband too is arrested in most of the cases and has to face humiliation in the society and also ill-treatment of the authorities.

These surveys and studies from various countries indicate that domestic violence among men at the hands of their wives or from their intimate partner is not uncommon. Appropriate provisions should be there to deal with domestic violence in a more neutral way.[1]

In a study of 1000 married men among the various age groups from 21-49 years of age in the rural villages of Haryana, 52.4% of males experience gender-based violence in India. 51.5% of males have experienced some sort of torture or violence at the hands of their wives or their intimate partners in their lifetime. 10.5% of males have experienced gender-based violence at the hands of their wives or intimate partners in the last 12 months. [2]

[1] Findlaw ~ domestic violence against men

[2]   https://www.aihw.gov.au/reports/domestic-violence/family-domestic-sexual-violence-in-australia-2018/contents/summary

Reasons why domestic violence cases against men go unreported

There are many reasons for which men often do not reveal the violence they face by their spouses or by their intimate partners.

1. General Stereotypes against males– Men often feel discriminated against or feel uneasy in opening up about the violence that they face because they feel ashamed that they will be judged and will be labelled as wimpy and effeminate. They think their struggle against violence will go in vain because of gender-specific laws and provisions that are given in the Indian Constitution. They feel that they have failed the role of protector in nurturing their families.

2. Fear of fake cases– Men often feel that revealing the violence can cause unnecessary nuisance and they do not want to face the legal consequences because of the gender-biased or gender-specific laws in our Constitution. They feel that they have to leave their families and they don't want to lose custody of their children which is often a cumbersome process.

3. Societal and family pressure– Most of the Indians continue to live with their families even after their marriage. Because of this factor, men feel ashamed of opening up about the violence. The society also plays a crucial role in nurturing gender biased laws and stereotypes against a particular gender.

4. Denial– Mostly people feel that domestic violence can only happen to a woman. And they live in denial when they get to know that man can also be a victim of domestic violence. So, basically, people never really want

to talk about it.

Maintenance of wife by the husband

Section 125 of the Code of Criminal Procedure, 1973 mentions that a person is supposed to maintain his wife, children and his parents who are unable to maintain themselves. Even if the wife earns, that income is not enough to support her and the husband has to provide for her needs.

Section 37 of the Special Marriage Act provides that the husband has to maintain his wife from his property after divorce until there is a change in her circumstances like she is remarried or has turned immoral.

Section 18of the Hindu Adoption and Maintenance Act states that a Hindu wife has a right to be maintained by her husband throughout her lifetime.

These all laws which are mentioned above provide for the maintenance of a wife by her husband but no provisions are there which talk about a husband being maintained by his wife. There may be a situation where the husband can also need maintenance but that criteria is not provided in the above-discussed provisions.

Even though the Hind Marriage Act appears to be gender-neutral but again all other laws such as Section 125 of CrPC, Hindu Marriage, and Adoption Act are still gender-biased and compels a duty upon only men to maintain his wife and children.

CHAPTER TEN

Sexual assault against men(non- centrical law)

According to the definition given by World Health Organization, child sexual abuse is the involvement of a child in sexual activity that he or she does not fully comprehend, is unable to give informed consent to, or that violates the laws or social taboos of society. There is an unending silence around this subject and a very large percentage of people feel that child sexual abuse happens only to girls[1]

When we compare the amount of information available on the internet, we will find that most of the information on this topic is related to sexual assault of women. This is because it is difficult to gather information on the experiences of men who have faced sexual assault at some point in their lives. If we search 'Rape in India' on Wikipedia, the first line itself talks only about the rape of women. It says, "Rape is the fourth most common crime against women in India." It is important to address the issue such as rape, but we also need to know that rape and sexual assault is a gender-neutral crime and happens to men too. Focusing merely on the problems faced by one gender and neglecting the problems of the other is not fair or just in any way. It is unjust and unfair for the males to suffer because of a false belief that they cannot be sexually harassed.

The Judgment by the Supreme Court that decriminalized the consensual sexual relations between adults of the same gender, which was a crime under Section 377 of the Indian Penal Code, is still looked down upon by many people in India who still consider homosexuality a taboo and a disease which means that the homosexuals still have a long road to travel in order to be empowered and given their rights. Therefore, in a country like India, where two years back, people were not even ready to accept homosexuality as a natural phenomenon and believed it to be a taboo, the idea of a male member of the society being raped, by any gender, still has a long way to go before it gets recognized by the people.

The question, "Are men and boys raped and sexually harassed too?" was asked in the questionnaire which had 115 responses. Out of 115, 107people agreed that men and boys can be sexually assaulted too, whereas, 8 people answered otherwise. 2 of them had their own opinion, which was, "In rare cases... 30-40 percent cases...But complaints are not recorded.", "Sometimes, not many times, as compared to women."[2]

According to the responses of the survey, sexual assault of men and boys exists, but it is not as common as sexual assault of women and girls. As is also written by one of the person who answered the survey, "sexual assault of men and boys happen sometimes, not many times as compared to women."

According to the Crime survey for England and Wales (CSEW), "in the year 2017, till the month of March, there were 20% women and 4% men who experienced sexual assault since the age of 16, equivalent to 3.4 million female and 631,000 male victims." [The Crime Survey for England and Wales (CSEW), About Sexual Violence, Rape Crisis England and Wales]53.9% believe that rape of men and boys is not an uncommon crime and it takes place more frequently than we are aware of, whereas, 45.2% believe that rape of men is not that common and is rare.

Even though women are more prone to sexual assault than men, it does not negate the fact that men and boys are sexually assaulted too and they should be given equal importance and opportunity to report the assault and get justice because sexual assault is a gender-neutral crime and there should be no discrimination on the basis of gender, which is also a Fundamental Right under Article 15 (1) of the Constitution of India. There needs to be acknowledgment that whatever happens with a woman can happen with a man too. If a woman can face sexual harassment at workplace, a man can too. If a boss who is of any gender, asks for sexual favours from an employee, irrespective of the gender, is committing sexual harassment at workplace and there are no exceptions if the employee does not do it willingly or does not agree to it. In the above given case study, there was no proof that A had done what was asked of him by his boss, yet some people answered that A did it willingly. This is because they presumed that since he was a man, he got an opportunity of getting sexual with a woman and he took it. Here, it is only 2 out of 115 people, but all over the world, there will be more out of 7.8 billion people.

[1]   https://www.urbandictionary.com/define.php?term=Toxic%20Masculinit

[2]   https://ccsindia.org/indias-law-should-recognise-men-can-be-raped-too

CHAPTER ELEVEN

Is "Rape is patriarchal" ?

Rape in general defined as the crime committed by men against women. It has been conceptualized as sexual victimization of women by male preparatory that manifest the rape-supportive patriarchial society. However, in reality, it has been found that there is a significant number of rapes and other sexual violence victims are male too but the mindset that rape cannot happen with men distanced these rape survivors from the research spotlight.

The rape of males is seen as taboo in the society which has a negative connotation among heterosexual men. The rape of males is always seen with the perspective of manliness and masculinity. Consequently, most of the victims feared to report sexual assault they experienced.

<u>Men are not Vulnerable</u>

In the male dominant society like India and Pakistan. Men are seen as the strongest of all because of which they are not supposed to do the things that go against their manliness, not even allowed to openly cry. This perception of society that men are strongest among human beings depicts that males cannot be raped nor even that they are vulnerable to it. These societies believe that only women can be raped.

<u>Men rape in Different countries</u>

In the UK, initially "Criminal Justice and Public Order Act, 1994" made changes in laws regarding rape that removed buggery from the statue and add the term "non-consensual anal as well as vaginal penile penetration". Through this act, it was for the first time effort was made to recognize the rape of males in the UK legal system.[1]

Later "Sexual Offences Act, 2003 (England and Wales)" redefined it further, to include even non-consensual penetration through the mouth and removed the vague provision of indecent assault. However, the definition of rape still requires penile penetration. Hence, rape laws of the UK are still not gender-neutral as women cannot be penalized for raping men as per the current definition.

In Scotland, the "Sexual Offences (Scotland) Act, 2009" brought serious changes in their rape laws and redefined it as:

The intentional or reckless penetration of the penis (to any extent) into the vagina, anus or mouth of another person, without that person consenting and without any reasonable belief that consent was obtained" Despite the changes in rape and sexual offences of these countries, there are still some countries like India, Pakistan where rape is continued to be seen as a gendered crime.

<u>Male Rape and Indian Laws</u>

In India rape is considered as the act of penile penetration, or any foreign object into the vagina without the consent of women or girl. Sec 375[2] of IPC mentions about rape as "sexual intercourse with a woman against her will, without her consent, by coercion, misrepresentation or fraud or at a time when she has been intoxicated or duped or is of unsound mental health and in any case, if she is under 18 years of age". If we analyse the definition then we find that it makes two clear, albeit subtle inferences:

- A rape offender is necessarily a man.
- A victim of rape is necessarily a woman.

Hence, the whole definition is considering the rape of only women and there's no clause for the rape of male. It manifests that in India there's no particular law if a male rapes another male or a female rapes a male. At, the most they can be sodomised under sec 377[3] of IPC that is modelled on Buggery Act, 1533 where unnatural sex is an "Act against god".[4] Except for this section, all other laws and sections are meant only for females. This Inequality in the treatment of rape of male from rape of female affecting the equalitarianism of our constitution. Though there's POCSO ("Protection of Children from Sexual Offences") for the sexual assault of male child such provision does not exist for an adult male. There's no reason, why instances of sexual assault on a male child are treated differently from a similar act committed against an adult male. If we made the provision for the rape of male child then why can't we make similar provision for men also? The basic idea behind it is men in India considered as invulnerable and as ones who use their power to exploit women. However if we consider the ground reality that is reflected in the survey of Insia Dariwala which surveyed 1500 male out of which 71% of men surveyed said they were abused, 84.9% said they had not told anyone about the abuse and The primary reasons for this were shame (55.6%), followed by confusion (50.9%), fear (43.5%) and guilt (28.7%).

[1] (PDF) The scope of male rape: A selective review of research, policy and practice

[2] Indian Penal Code 1860, Sec 375

[3] Indian Penal Code 1860, Sec 377

[4] Rituparna Chatterjee, "The mindset is that boys are not raped": India ends silence on male sex abuse, The Guardian, May 23, 2018, https://www.theguardian.com/global-development/2018/may/23/indian-study-male-sexual-abuse-film-maker-insia-dariwala Gazala Parveen, "Ought The Rape/Sexual Assault Law In India

CHAPTER TWELVE

Gender Neutrality of Rape Laws

The 172nd law commission of India in March 2000 recommended that rape laws in India should be made gender-neutral to protect male victims too. The underlying principle behind it is a presumption that offence of rape will be desexualized and the stigma attached to it will vanish. However, the government did not act to implement the suggestions. Later in 2017, a PIL was filed at the Delhi High Court by adv. Sanjiv Kumar, which challenged the constitutionality of the rape laws under the Indian Penal Code (IPC). In his petition he stated:

"Gender neutrality is a simple recognition of reality — men sometimes fall victim to the same or at least very similar acts to those suffered by women...Male rape is far too prevalent to be termed as an anomaly or a freak incident. By not having gender-neutral rape laws, we are denying a lot more men justice than is commonly thought."

On the same reasoning on July 2019 KTS Tulsi, a senior lawyer and Parliamentarian in the Rajya Sabha also brought a gender-neutral bill ("Criminal Law Amendment Bill, 2019") before parliament to make the rape laws gender-neutral in India. As per him:

"Law needs to be balanced. The balance has been disturbed. All sexual offences should be gender-neutral. Men, women, and other genders can be perpetrators and also victims of these offences. Men, women and others need to be protected."

The basic idea behind the bill is to propose necessary changes in Indian Penal Code (IPC), the Criminal procedure Code and the Indian Evidence Act so that the gender-specific words like "any man" and "any woman" likewise, mentioned in 354A, 354B, 354C, 354D, 375 and 376 of IPC to be replaced by gender-neutral words like "any person". This would provide protections to all gender i.e women, men and transgender. Addition to it also talks about the insertion of sec 375A in the IPC that defines sexual assault as "intentionally touches the genitals, anus or breast of the person or makes the person touch the vagina, penis, anus or breast of that person or any other person, without the other person's consent except where such touching is carried out for proper hygienic or medical purposes." This section ensures that not only inappropriate touching of female parts constitute sexual assault but inappropriate touching of the male part also constitutes it. Further, this bill also calls for the insertion of section 8A in section 354 of IPC which defines modesty

Women's Sexual Purity Is More Important than Men's

Linked to the idea that men have an uncontrollable sex drive is the idea that women do not have a strong sex drive and should be, in some ways, protected from sex. Traditional views held that a woman's worth was determined, at least in part, by her sexual purity and that rape was wrong, either fully, or in part, because it led to a loss of honour for the raped woman's family or community, and/or to the loss of the woman's monetary value to her father.

Judgments

Dr N.G. Dastane v S Dastane

In this case, the Supreme Court held that although it is supposed that the one who is stronger commits physical cruelty towards the other i.e. a husband toward his wife. But women, as well as men both, are capable of causing mental cruelty towards their partners.

Rajesh Sharma & others v State of Bihar

In this case, the court laid down certain directions to prevent the misuse of Section 498-A of IPC. The court gave directions to set up a Family Welfare Committee in each district by District Legal Services Authority and to look into the cases of domestic violence reported under Section 498-A of IPC for a month before making any arrest. The Committee would comprise para legal volunteers, social workers, retired persons who should be given basic training for doing the task.

Mamta Namdeo v. Ghanshyam Bihari

In Mamta Namdeo v. Ghanshyam Bihari Namdeo, AIR 2013 CHH. 89 case, the couple were married as per Hindu Rites sometime in June 1994. During this period, four children were born from the wedlock, out of which one has died and three are alive and living with their father. According to the husband, she expressed unwillingness to live with him, as she wanted to marry another person. She was in habit of abusing, misbehaving and threatening to inflict in false criminal cases including dowry cases. Then they started to live in separate rooms and then he was forced to file a divorce petition.

CHAPTER THIRTEEN

How men can cloak?

Men, because of toxic masculinity and their stereotyped upbringing that men are not soft, are believed to be the more aggressive gender than women. Even though it is likely that all the genders respond and cope up with sexual assault and rape similarly, that is, suicidal, shame, guilt, depression, trauma, fear, confusion, self-blame, etc, men are more likely to become more aggressive and respond towards such incidents through anger than women. This not only affects them but also their whole family and people close to them because this anger is sometimes taken out on them. They become frustrated because it is difficult for them to comprehend what happened to them, and most importantly, how is it possible that something like that happened to a man like himself who was always made to believe that he is strong and manly and nothing as such can happen to him. Male victims of rape and sexual assault are also more prone to become addicts and alcoholics. They may start feeling that they are not man enough or there could be fear of homosexuality.

"Male physiological reactions during a sexual assault may also make it more difficult for a male survivor to recognize that he was sexually assaulted. Some men may have an erection or may ejaculate during a sexual assault, and may later feel confused that perhaps this means that they enjoyed the experience, or that others will not believe that they were sexually assaulted. In reality, erections and ejaculations may be purely physiological responses, sometimes caused by intense fear or pain. In fact, some perpetrators will deliberately manipulate their victim to orgasm, out of a desire to completely control their victims. The perpetrator can continue this manipulation after the assault to coerce the survivor away from reporting or seeking help. A physical reaction of an erection or ejaculation during a sexual assault in no way indicates that the man enjoyed the experience or that he did something to cause it or permit it."

The legislations which are women-centric in nature and are inflexible should be examined properly to remove any loopholes if present in them.

There is a need to protect women so no harm is there in making women-centric laws but the point to be kept in mind is that if any legislation is made to help the women victims it should not destroy an innocent male's life. The legislation should be made keeping the rights of both males and females in mind.

The dowry laws are strictly implemented against the groom's family but still, there are cases related to the same. The reason for its existence is that only the people who take dowry are punished and not the bride's family who is giving dowry which is also a crime under the Dowry Prohibition Act. Mostly, the people who give dowry are the ones who ask for dowry. So it is necessary that the laws are properly implemented.

CHAPTER FOURTEEN

Conclusions

It is an accepted academic stand that sexism is systematic and structural, and that it involves the subordination of one group as a whole by another group which enjoys power and advantage in the system. The locus of sexism is primarily in the system of framework, not in the particular act. It is the patriarchal system itself which places the extra responsibilities on the male, and it may be the price that same men are paying for their overall advantageous position in the society. However, one must agree that the overall greater severity of the first sexism (sexism against women) does not imply that the second sexism (sexism against men) should be denied, ignored or tolerated. Some new cases like Lucknow case of cab driver and many other when women assault or we can say torture men and, sexual assault and rape and the stereotype that rape is patriarchal and can happen only to women and girls because men are strong and cannot be victims of such crimes. The toxic mentality of the society needs to be changed and the truth should be revealed to everyone and the sooner it is done, the better

Women – orientated laws are made to protect women from abuses in society. It was the need when they were implemented and still the need exists. But along with it, it is also necessary to see that no one who is innocent is getting harmed by such laws in any war whatsoever. Also, a tedious job in the hand of the judges to see that the approach of the society that the women are the ones who are always the victims in women-centric laws should not affect them when they are delivering their judgment

With regards to the existence of both male and female survivors, the US's Centers for Disease Control in Atlanta has estimated that 18.3% of American women and 1.4% of American men have experienced rape at some point in their lives. Both percentages are likely to be underestimated due to stigma attached to reporting the crime. Law should not be bias , as constitution gives rights to the people but with restrictions, same applies for laws made of women there should be some restrictions to cub the misuse of women centric laws .

www.ingramcontent.com/pod-product-compliance
Lightning Source LLC
Chambersburg PA
CBHW050623160726
48003CB00003B/1301